THIS BOOK BELONGS TO

_____

Please Read;
In Defense of Thomas
Jefferson.

THOMAS JEFFERSON

NOTEBOOK

CIDER MILL PRESS

BOOK
PUBLISHERS
KENNEBUNKPORT, MAINE

Foreword

Thomas Jefferson and the Power of Words

BY R. B. BERNSTEIN, AUTHOR OF *THOMAS JEFFERSON* AND *THE FOUNDING FATHERS RECONSIDERED*

In the spring of 1825, Thomas Jefferson penned a letter that explained the purpose of a document he had drafted in the summer of 1776. As the "Sage of Monticello," Jefferson answered letters from friends and foes, historians and biographers, anyone who sought his attention. This time, he was writing to Henry Lee ("Light-Horse Harry Lee"), a hero of the American Revolution, about his intent in drafting the Declaration of independence:

This was the object of the Declaration of Independence. Not to find out new principles, or new arguments, never before thought of, not merely to say things which had never been said before; but to place before mankind the common sense of the subject, in terms so plain and firm as to command their assent, and to justify ourselves in the independent stand we are compelled to take. Neither aiming at originality of principle or sentiment, nor yet copied from any particular and previous writing, it was intended to be an expression of the American mind, and to give to that expression the proper tone and spirit called for by the occasion.

Expressing the "American mind" – a term that he may have coined – was essential to Jefferson throughout his career; he took great pride in believing that he had done so in imperishable terms.

Jefferson saw the American Revolution as a revolution of ideas and fought it on that basis. Others drew swords or shouldered muskets to defend American independence and constitutional rights, but a small group of brilliant, contentious men defined what America meant, what independence meant, what rights meant, and how Americans could secure their independence and rights. Jefferson stood out among them. First, he was a Virginian, a citizen of the largest, wealthiest, and most powerful of the original thirteen states. John Adams cited two other reasons: Jefferson's "happy talent for composition" and his "peculiar felicity of expression." Jefferson was famed for being an expert, reliable, and effective legislative draftsman. When the Second Continental Congress had to end eleven years of constitutional argument with Great Britain, the task of drafting that statement naturally fell to him.

Justifying the Americans in declaring independence would have been achievement enough. What made the Declaration truly remarkable was Jefferson's defining what independence was *for* – what goals the new nation's government, politics, and laws should have and how they should reshape American society. Addressing the American need to become a truly independent nation with its face to the future, Jefferson recast the Revolution as not just a vital event for his countrymen but as a model for everyone. Americans, he insisted, were leading the way for the human race. This theme governed his extraordinary, multifaceted career and his writing for the rest of his life.

Whether as a revolutionary advocate, a constitution-crafter and lawmaker, a diplomat, Secretary of State, Vice President, President, or elder statesman, Jefferson was at his best with his pen in his hand and a grand subject before him. He took the lead in drafting the era's most revolutionary statute, the Virginia Statute for Religious Freedom, defining and justifying the principle of strict separation of church and state; he wrote the most important American book before 1800, *Notes on the State of Virginia*; he fought for free public education and created two of the great American educational institutions, West Point and the University of Virginia. Even though he offered tortured justifications for slavery and the racial inferiority of the enslaved, he also defined the standards of liberty and equality by which we judge him wanting for owning slaves and for defending slavery.

Jefferson's political and governmental labor over his lifetime filled thousands of pages of letters, memoranda, bills and statutes, speeches and other writings, each bearing the unique stamp of his thought and literary skill. We argue over liberty and equality, government power and limits on that power, issues of church and state, and the power and value of education, in terms that Jefferson's thought and writings shaped.

The creation of the United States was an act of literary creation as much as political or military struggle. One reason why so many Americans and people around the world study Jefferson is that he not only thought creatively about the enduring challenges of liberty and government, but did so in elegant, lucid prose. He may well be the finest politician-writer that America ever produced. Only Lincoln rivals him in this regard. In the quotations gathered in this handsome volume's pages, we can follow Jefferson's efforts to order the world with words.

Introduction

by MATTHEW ELIOT, AUTHOR OF *THE WIT
AND WISDOM OF OUR TROOPS*

*O*ne of America's greatest presidents. One of its foremost intellectuals. One of its best writers. Like a number of his contemporaries, the achievements of Thomas Jefferson are staggering, and even more so to us, who reside in this era of specialization and seemingly constant activity.

How did he do it? How could one man build a nation, construct a democratic ideology potent enough to bear fruit more than 200 years later, and also manage to excel in philosophy, law, architecture, linguistics, horticulture, and mathematics?

It was not just genius. That is a part of it, certainly, but the achievements of America's third president exceed even the most brilliant, and ambitious, historical personages. Instead, it was pairing his undeniable genius with a wide-ranging and insatiable curiosity, an insistent search for truth, and the ability to grant weight and value to those thoughts and phenomena most would categorize as insignificant.

This last quality is no minor thing. For while Jefferson's innate brilliance is rare, his devotion to a careful consideration of the world is available to everyone. And it may prove to be the most transformative, and illuminating, of all his features. Were he not so willing to believe that each individual and occurrence had something valuable to offer, it is unlikely that a man of such considerable talents would ever believe "that all men are created equal," never mind believe it with such intensity that he would pin the hopes of a fledgling nation upon it.

Jefferson was such an enthusiast for details and information that the very first thing he did each day was patrol the grounds of Monticello and record his various observations onto a notebook consisting of ivory leaves—observations that would later be transcribed in one of seven notebooks that he maintained. Once this transfer had been made, the ivory notebook would be erased in preparation for the next morning's investigations. This willingness to capture, and the ability to organize, is a vital part of any great intellectual's process.

But it is not enough to simply collect and catalogue one's thoughts. Jefferson's outsized impact on the political and intellectual life of this nation is also due to his dedicated writing practice—the massive amount of time spent translating his impressions and observations into something more substantial. Surprisingly, one of history's great men, one of the most active and lively and curious individuals the world has ever seen, admitted to spending the majority of the day confined to his desk: "From sun-rise to one or two o'clock, I am drudging at the writing table." So devoted was he to this regimen that later in his life he utilized dumbbells to strengthen his hands and wrists, and employed a special cushion to support his wrists in their considerable labors.

While that type of commitment is not an option for many of us, Jefferson's lifelong involvement with close observation and written elaboration provides a valuable lesson to all. We may never change the world or inscribe our names and ideas upon it. But we can, if we are dedicated to esteem this world and the products of our mind, if we regard them as worthy of recognition and reflection, infuse our lives with the meaning and depth we yearn for. Through his unwavering practice, Jefferson shows us that the making of many small marks can add up to something grand and seemingly impossible, provided one is willing to look back and reckon with them.

Prior to Lewis and Clark's famous expedition into the American West, Jefferson gave these instructions to his close friend and former secretary, Captain Meriwether Lewis: "Your observations are to be taken with great pains & accuracy to be entered distinctly, & intelligibly for others as well as yourself, to comprehend all the elements necessary."

If one steps back and looks at the whole of his life, it feels like Jefferson is asking us to do the same, providing us with a glimpse of what is possible if we can make ourselves believe that those small bits we are offered are exceedingly precious, and worthy of chronicling.

Page from the Original Rough Draught of the Declaration of Independence (June 1776)

A Declaration by the Representatives of the UNITED STATES
OF AMERICA, in General Congress assembled.

When in the course of human events it becomes necessary for one people to
dissolve the political bands which have connected them with another, and to
assume among the powers of the earth the separate and equal station to
which the laws of nature & of nature's god entitle them, a decent respect
to the opinions of mankind requires that they should declare the causes
which impel them to the separation.

We hold these truths to be self-evident; that all men are
created equal; that they are endowed by their creator with
inherent & inalienable rights; among these are the
life & liberty, & the pursuit of happiness; that to secure these ends, governments are instituted among men, deriving their just powers from
the consent of the governed; that whenever any form of government
shall becomes destructive of these ends, it is the right of the people to alter
or to abolish it, & to institute new government, laying it's foundation on
such principles & organising it's powers in such form, as to them shall
seem most likely to effect their safety & happiness. prudence indeed
will dictate that governments long established should not be changed for
light & transient causes: and accordingly all experience hath shewn that
mankind are more disposed to suffer while evils are sufferable, than to
right themselves by abolishing the forms to which they are accustomed. but
when a long train of abuses & usurpations [begun at a distinguished period
&] pursuing invariably the same object, evinces a design to reduce
them under absolute Despotism, it is their right, it is their duty, to throw off such
government & to provide new guards for their future security. such has
been the patient sufferance of these colonies; & such is now the necessity
which constrains them to expunge their former systems of government.
the history of the present king of Great Britain is a history of unremitting injuries and
usurpations, [among which appears no solitary fact to contra-
dict the uniform tenor of the rest all of which have] in direct object the
establishment of an absolute tyranny over these states. to prove this, let facts be
submitted to a candid world [for the truth of which we pledge a faith
yet unsullied by falsehood]

The whole art of
government consists in

THE ART OF
BEING HONEST.

— *A Summary View of the Rights of British America* (1774)

God is invisible and
yet performs all miracle.

We all Know that a person
can learn about Life without
Religion.

Hebrew as SheKhinal—
light or radiance)
form the halos around
around angels & the luminous
joy in the face of a saint

Judeo-Christian tradition

Miracles and angels defy reason.

Thomas Jefferson

On every question of construction,

CARRY
OURSELVES
BACK

to the time when the constitution
was adopted...

— Letter to William Johnson (June 12, 1823)

Mount Rushmore

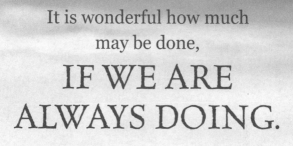

It is wonderful how much
may be done,

IF WE ARE
ALWAYS DOING.

—Letter to Martha Jefferson (May 5, 1787)

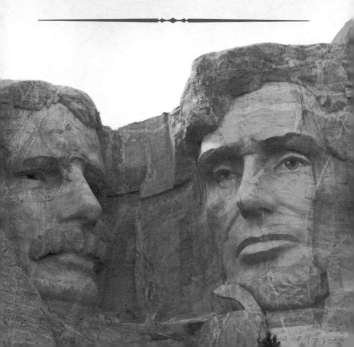

No society is

SO PRECIOUS

as that of one's own family.

— Letter to Randolph Jefferson (January 11, 1789)

Thomas Jefferson Memorial during the Cherry Blossom Festival in Washington, DC

The wise know their weakness
too well to assume infallibility;

AND HE WHO
KNOWS MOST,

knows best how little
he knows.

—Batture Pamphlet (February 25, 1812)

ONLY AIM TO DO YOUR DUTY,

and mankind will give you credit where you fail.

— A Summary View of the Rights of British America (1774)

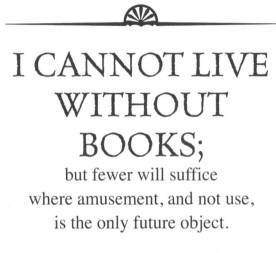

I CANNOT LIVE WITHOUT BOOKS;

but fewer will suffice
where amusement, and not use,
is the only future object.

—Letter to John Adams (June 10, 1815)

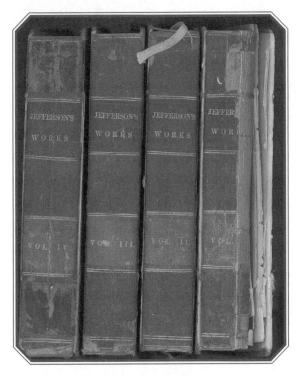

Jefferson's Works

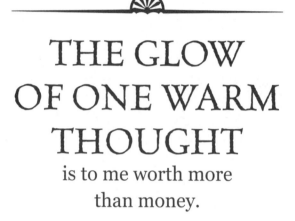

THE GLOW
OF ONE WARM
THOUGHT
is to me worth more
than money.

— Letter to Charles McPherson (February 25, 1773)

Writing the Declaration of Independence, 1776

Be good, be learned, &
BE INDUSTRIOUS.

—Letter to Peter Carr (August 10, 1787)

Thomas Jefferson statue near the Museum d'Orsay in Paris

Thomas Jefferson, Roger Sherman, Benjamin Franklin,
Robert Livingston, and John Adams, 1776

Where the press is free,

AND EVERY MAN ABLE TO READ,

all is safe.

— Letter to Charles Yancey (January 6, 1816)

Although a republican
government is slow to move,

YET WHEN ONCE
IN MOTION,
its momentum becomes
irresistible.

—Letter to Francis C. Gray (March 4, 1815)

Determine never to be idle.

—Letter to Martha Jefferson (May 5, 1787)

Thomas Jefferson holding a Declaration of Independence

THE GOOD
OPINION
OF MANKIND,
like the lever of Archimedes,
with the given fulcrum,

MOVES
THE WORLD.

—Letter to M. Corrêa da Serra (December 27, 1814)

The study in Thomas Jefferson's Monticello home,
Charlottesville, Virginia

I have not observed men's honesty to increase

WITH THEIR RICHES.

—Letter to Jeremiah Moore (August 14, 1800)

Thomas Jefferson closeup on the two-dollar bill

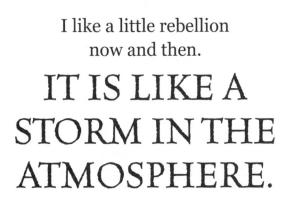

I like a little rebellion
now and then.

IT IS LIKE A
STORM IN THE
ATMOSPHERE.

—Letter to Abigail Adams (February 22, 1787)

The greatest good
we can do our country
is to heal its party
divisions and

MAKE
THEM ONE
PEOPLE.

—Letter to John Dickinson (July 23, 1801)

Thomas Jefferson's home, Monticello

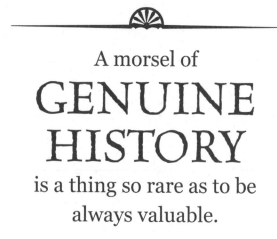

A morsel of

GENUINE HISTORY

is a thing so rare as to be always valuable.

—Letter to John Adams (September 8, 1817)

Honesty is the first chapter in the

BOOK OF WISDOM.

—Letter to Nathaniel Macon (January 12, 1819)

THE
BOISTEROUS
SEA OF LIBERTY

is never without a wave.

—Letter to Richard Rush (October 20, 1820)

*"Independence Declared 1776," with bust portraits
of the first eight presidents*

Page from the Original Rough Draught of the Declaration of Independence (June 1776)

has refused his assent to laws the most wholesome and necessary for the pub-
-lic good:

has forbidden his governors to pass laws of immediate & pressing importance,
unless suspended in their operation till his assent should be obtained;
and when so suspended, he has neglected utterly to attend to them.

has refused to pass other laws for the accommodation of large districts of people
unless those people would relinquish the right of representation in the legislature; a right
inestimable to them, & formidable to tyrants only:

he has called together legislative bodies at places unusual [illegible]
[illegible] only firmness his invasions on the rights of the people:
dissolved, he has refused for a long time after such dissolutions to cause others to be elected;   [& on their deaths]
whereby the legislative powers, incapable of annihilation, have returned to
the people at large for their exercise, the state remaining in the mean time
exposed to all the dangers of invasion from without & convulsions within:

has endeavored to prevent the population of these states; for that purpose
obstructing the laws for naturalization of foreigners; refusing to pass others
to encourage their migrations hither, & raising the conditions of new ap-
-propriations of lands:

has suffered the administration of justice totally to cease in some of these
states refusing his assent to laws for establishing judiciary powers:

has made our judges dependant on his will alone, for the tenure of their offices,
the [+] & payment and amount of their salaries: [+ Dr Franklin]

has erected a multitude of new offices [by a self-assumed power] & sent hit
their swarms of officers to harrass our people & eat out their substance:

has kept among us in times of peace, standing armies [& ships of war] without the consent of our legislature

has affected to render the military, independent of & superior to the civil power:

has combined with others to subject us to a jurisdiction foreign to our constitution
-tions and unacknoleged by our laws; giving his assent to their pretended acts of
legislation, for quartering large bodies of armed troops among us;

for protecting them by a mock-trial from punishment for any murders
which they should commit on the inhabitants of these states;

for cutting off our trade with all parts of the world;

for imposing taxes on us without our consent;

for depriving us in many cases of the benefits of trial by jury;

for transporting us beyond seas to be tried for pretended offences:
for abolishing the free system of English laws in a neighboring province, establishing therein an arbitrary

About Cider Mill Press
Book Publishers

Good ideas ripen with time. From seed to harvest,
Cider Mill Press brings fine reading, information,
and entertainment together between the covers of
its creatively crafted books. Our Cider Mill bears
fruit twice a year, publishing a new crop of titles
each spring and fall.

Visit us on the web at
www.cidermillpress.com
or write to us at
PO Box 454
12 Spring Street
Kennebunkport, Maine 04046